AUTOBIOGRAPHY OF AN OCEAN

a.g.

To the Guru...

who said what had to be said, before I entered this life..

that which I heard only after he departed...

yet, we meet here...

PROLOGUE

**Today, what appears as *the Ocean*,
once it was just a bubble floating on water**

Or so it believed...

Because, before that it was a tiny droplet, too afraid to go anywhere. Too tiny to even get noticed.

Or so it believed....

Because, much before that, it was a mud-ball, that often had a regular shape, though it changed easily, as it happens to the mud-balls. And it lived in a group of fellow mud-balls. Life was simple and full of aims. There was much meaning in existence. And there was a grand goal!!

Or so it believed....

Because, it has memories of being a porcelain figure for a very long time. With a regular shape. And even a name! Oh, and not just once, that happened many times. Though in those times, it carried no memory of any of the previous shapes and any of those previous names.

Maybe, it starts with the story of a porcelain doll. Beautiful, shapely, graceful and talented! It was intelligent, presentable, and funny at times; and it often used to dream in the colours of the rainbow! What a delightful eventful world it lived in.

Or so it believed....

SECTION 1

Story of the Porcelain doll

♦ ♦ ♦

CHAPTER 1

It was a small hamlet of a town, where I came to senses. A dull-white plain and simple doll of porcelain, rough and naturally textured, living in a small family of similar folks. I had a name given and we all had faces, that expressed true emotions, often raw and unsophisticated, but all too natural. We had a few things at home, usually just enough to manage living, and rest we cobbled up with our imagination, that was too wild and creative, so in a sense, our house was full of some real and a whole lot of imaginary stuff. We even had memorable events around something that originally came out of one member's imagination, and a whole bunch of such historic nostalgia actually. Those collective memories were truly what made us feel like a close-knit family, the best of its kind actualy.

There were quite a few other doll folks too. All with names and faces. All with their shapes and qualities. Some of them lived close-by, so we knew each other intimately. Others too were known to all, but not so closely. But we knew everyone, one way or other. All were the same dull-white plain and simple dolls of porcelain, rough and naturally textured. You saw one and you knew where it came from, but soon you'd forget anything specific about them.

Life was simple, in fact. There were no surprises of any kind, so we pretended to create some, just to have fun. Our roles in life were kind of fixed, and as far as we could see in time, our futures were fixed too. But that was a good thing, since it took away any anxiety about life's events. Knowing the lives of predecessors, elders always knew what lay ahead and they shared this knowledge whenever we fell into dilemma. Life repeated in every next generation, going through the same motions, same events, same challenges and same few options. Though every event initially seemed to bring a new situation, but those were indeed a few sparse moments, since soon we knew it was a reoccurance of such kind of events and then realise that indeed we knew whatever was there to be known about life. There were no unknowns.

Only till I tasted the thrill of wading in the unknown!

Chinook and Hatra were my constant buddies. There were others too – Ulgra, Timbro, Intok, Amphil. Oh, they were all so funny and spontaneous. Most of the time we were together, playing pranks on others or simply inventing our own private games. But Chinook and Hatra were special to me. Chinook was always in trouble! Someone or other would hurt the feelings or rub too closely to scratch the delicate porcelain body. It is astonishing how frequently and regularly such incidents happened. Somehow, I considered it my duty, rather responsibility, to look after Chinook. It was beyond my imagination how Chinook could survive without my care. We had that special bonding and most were aware of it. Being useful and helpful to one was often enough to fill me with a nice feeling about myself.

But Hatra was different. With Hatra around, I always felt naughty and full of life! Not that I wanted to cause any hurt or bad feelings. I think Hatra too enjoyed my silly pranks and fully participated in them by remaining deliberately ignorant of what was impending. I'm sure the whole sequence was pretty obvious, as everyone else stepped aside or played their imagined role, to let me complete the charade as planned. My buddies never spoiled these pranks and that might be a big reason we hung around for so long. At least that's how it appeared to me.

One advantage of living in the plains is that there are no large geographical features to make us wonder what lay beyond them. And everything in sight was easily reachable and known. Like the fixed pace of the town-clock, everything and everyone were always in their designated place, well known and totally predictable. Before the day began, we knew what was in store and it was always so. So, we learnt to invent dreams that were fantastic and wonderful. It was fun to discuss them with others, but never with enough pull to get lived.

Hatra was the one who made me think about living some of my dreams. My dreams were perhaps biggest reason why this bunch of friends were interested in keeping close, as their dreams were generally of usual stuff, stories where you knew the end even before the plot unfoled. My dreams were too fantastic for them to relate, though they did enjoy the narrative. Hatra sensed that my heart was showing me these dreams as a future plan and of course, it wasn't remotely possible to live them in our small hamlet. I was torn between my concerns for wellbeing of Chinook and the direction of dreams that Hatra motivated me to explore.

As it happens, hope scored resounding victory over the practical, and I left for the big urban jungle. Big dreams need a very large place to come true, so I thought. And I was willing to pay whatever price it took, without having any idea what all it will take. The unknown stirred a myriad of emotions in my trembling heart, every step as heavy as those logs we carried, yet, the charm of living up those dreams was far too delicious to ignore.

It was a new feeling in me, fear all over, but I was feeling very alive. Like a warrior who steps out to conquer life!

CHAPTER 2

City was indeed far beyond anything I had imagined. It was a huge expanse of millions of dwellings and full of millions of others porcelain doll folks, though they were called people here, since most of them didn't seem to have any name and often no face as well. Curiously, everyone had attractive coloured patterns on them and they were covered in a sort of metallic glaze that had brilliant reflections and made them look ravishing with fine cuts and crisp edges. I felt rather raw looking amongst them and often got excluded from their company, which caused many scratches on my porcelain self. It was lonely and depressing, till I figured out how to get colours and that metallic glaze that not only looked brilliant but also saved from getting scratched in any manner.

Soon I was one amongst those city people, colourful, glazed in metallic shine, with fine cuts and crisp edges. Millions of people with millions of dreams, often just the same as mine. Well, with few variations of course. And we were all running, all the time, to chase our dreams. It was all so exciting for me, coming from a sleepy countryside where we always knew what was going to happen, as nothing much ever happened there. City never slept, it seems!

Of the few faces I saw often, Posha was the first one who even had a name. After weeks of initial hesitations and niceties that we put up around strangers, we decided to bunk up together. But it turned out that in a sense, we were no strangers. We hailed from similar hamlets, had similar bunch of friends and somewhat similar fantastic dreams. Well, not that strange actually, that we were similar in our spirit. In fact almost everyone we met had a similar past, and so it first became an invaluable aid to reveal our real selves and connect deeply, but sometimes it also turned into a weapon to attack each other, as we were too deeply aware of each other's weaknesses and mediocrity, being one ourselves.

We also gathered a few more names with faces and met up often to share our experiences of running behind the dreams. City had a lot of variety to offer, with many attractive locations, tastefully done-up diners, colourful lights and a huge variety of foods and drinks from all over the world. We never had a dull moment from whatever remained after our daily running. In fact, city even didn't force one to stay put with the same relationships. When you got disillusioned with one friend's reality, you can always find a new one and once againpretend being a different persona with different reality, only till one could figure out other's reality, which was often just the same as self, and yet it didn't compell to continue, rather it propelled to move on to another. Swiftly. Without any level of remorse or throwbacks. In this war, no one stopped to count the wounded.

City aided you with unlimited opportunities to pretend being someone else, someone much better, much superior, and much more polished than the real self. It helped you dream new dreams every day, those tiny dreams which all looked and felt different but were actually around the same theme, just with different actors. And when you got tired or bored of your own dreams, you can easily borrow others' dreams and align your life accordingly. In fact, after switching my dreams for a few times, I realized dreaming itself was a skill that can put your life on an altogether different platform! And then I was secretly ashamed of the petty dreams I carried from the hamlet. There was just so much more, so much richer and colourful and sophisticated material to incorporate into your dreams, that one life may be too short to achieve and live all that. Life seamed to have a purpose and a direction to go in.

Life was exciting as it became a constant roller-coaster of experiences, both at physical level and at emotional level. City never required you to get too close to anyone, not even to yourself. Freedom in all aspects of living, to present self as we want, eat what we want, dress-up as we fancy and the best, ignore everyone as if there is no other. There was so much to do, so many things to see and experience, so many attractions that it was easy to forget the crowd. And yourself. Festivals had their own charm, religious or imaginary. Well, in a way they were always around an imagined excuse, but celebrations had a running similarity. As if everyone wanted to drown in the cacophony and glitters. Sometimes it left me wondering what inner voices we are trying to bury under all this noise.

First one to crack was Antro and it came almost as a shock to all of us, though privately each one of us was struggling constantly and trying not to crack up. Or at least not appear as cracked up. Was it the shared destiny of all those who carry big dreams to the city? As if dreams were delicate eggs that are waiting to get trampled. Well, not always, since Antro actually achieved all that was in the original dreams, and some more of the borrowed dreams. Actually a lot more. At least that's how it appeared to the rest of us. And all of us fell into deep thoughts around our half-baked dream-lives and forever impending cracking moment.

We knew we were constantly running. We knew that we were adding more milestones ahead as we crossed the old ones. But none of us knew where we were reaching ultimately. At least none of us stopped long enough to dive so deep in ourselves. Perhaps that's where city puts a limit to your freedom, to not let you escape away from its magical lure, either anywhere far off or to somewhere dark within. At least for not long enough. And by the time such moment arrives, you have nowhere else to go, as original roots had dried up long before, for want to regular watering. Luckily, I still had some threads of the roots alive, must be accidently since I never truly tried to invest in them.

Perhaps I just needed a nudge and that was given by Nicto, who was always a keen observed of the unconscious. Trip to the hometown sounded therapeutic and nostalgic in the same measure, when Nicto suggested one evening. Just knowing that you have a safe place to go back, a place you can even call your roots, was a relief in itself. I was a bit tired from the constant thrill of the city that still remained largely an unknown to me, so the idea of taking a break into the forever-unsurprising-lifestyle at the hamlet was hugely appealing. Yet, I felt so hollow while going back. I wasn't the same person who came from the hamlet, since I outgrew those old dreams long back and switched for newer dreams many times over, what was there now to connect me to old pals? It was just a tiny hope that at least they would contain the same warmth and bonding, as nothing much really changed in the hamlet.

Though it was supposed to be a short break, underneath was also a proud desire to show off my new learnings and glazed city persona to my rustic friends, who must be undoubtedly still the same, stuck into a time warp.

Or so I thought...

◆ ◆ ◆

CHAPTER 3

It wasn't those many years since I went to the city and villages don't really change that much with time, and so proved the first looks as I reached the hamlet. Although, the place seemed to have shrunk drastically, became much poorer in appearance and dramatically dulled up in appearance. Or was it just my 'city eyes' making a fool of me. It was all just the same as ever!

I walked the streets at my usual 'city pace' and almost bumped into the house door, as it wasn't used to fast walkers or to those in a rush. I forgot that these streets weren't long enough to cover even if you walked backwards, as we often used to do. Time seemed to come to a halt, not moving at all, as all that was approachable was well within few leisurely paces. Hours didn't rush through, nor did minutes run past. Even seconds meandered for a while, before reluctantly ticking away. Life in the hamlet is more in the mind than at a geography.

After an eternity of an afternoon spent reminiscing the entire past spent there, many times over, arrived a bleak evening, with somewhat vague promise of catching up with the old gang. Intok and Amphil were easiest to locate, right where they always were, lurking at the coffee-shop besides the broken wall of ancient ruins. They even looked the same, maybe with an extra layer or two over them. I was suddenly aware of how unglazed, rough they were in their appearance. Eyes went painfully over those textured faces that once were our daily delight. But their same old jolly smiles washed away sins of the visual and life seemed to have come to a full circle. Or maybe not.

Apparently, they were whiling away life by living on what their families were producing from the fields and simply doling in the dusty by-lanes of the hamlet. That's how I saw them, though in their own words they were enjoying life. But Ulgra and Timbro were in much bad shape, according to them, though it sounded like progress to my ears. Each had joined their respective religious community and risen high in local politics, to an extent that they can't be eye to eye anymore. I found it very hard to believe, but then, they had simply filled the shoes left empty upon demise of the elderly. There are truly no surprises in this land of the predictable!

My mind was looking for any news of Chinook, one that I cared for a while and always thought about. It isn't surprising that I was often looking for a similar kind of friend while in the city! Does having someone to care for, also becomes integral part of who we are?

Hamlets are indeed an expert when it comes to hiding any bad news. When no one is showing any interest to discuss someone or something, truly a tragedy had occurred. Especially the kind which gnaws at the collective conscience of the populace. There are truly no 'others' in a hamlet, everyone is a part of everyone's being, and so the joys and sorrows and guilt are all felt equally. Should I too feel guilty of letting Chinook wither away, uncared and un-loved? Well, my newly acquired city glaze was much more slippery and smooth for such a tiny matter to stick easily. City folks move on in life, without wasting time looking back on the unpleasant. Perhaps I should look for my old heartbeat, my dearest, Hatra!

Only after going away did I truly realise how deeply I craved for the moments spent around Hatra. Was hard to figure out what it was that made me miss Hatra so much, though the thrill of fully executing a prank would be the most prominent experience. Then again, was I missing Hatra or the 'me' who was enjoying those self-satisfying dramatics? Was that the dearest part of 'me', that I cher-ished most and secretly wanted to extend over the whole life?

Dilemma vanished soon as I met Hatra in that tiny house, raising a small family of little ones, caring for the elders and going through the daily grind with a surrendered atti-tude towards life or whatever we meant by it. Hatra had almost no emotion or surprise, save the faint recognition of a long forgotten curio, one of those real and imaginary things we used to fill up our deprived lives with, in child-hood. Hatra and I were like standing at the far banks of a very wide river, which had no bridge into the past or pre-sent, except whatever remained in my memory. Perhaps, it was only the youthful moments spent together that I missed most, which had no existence by themselves and were totally unbelievable in this time. It was clear that I wasn't anywhere in Hatra's life, now or ever. And then it dawned on me that even Hatra wasn't anywhere in my life, now or ever. Just a passing fantasy that had its chance to deliver a few drops of delightful juice, if only in imagination. To think that I was calling these as my roots!

A day passed like a month and I lost my entire past in those slowly meandering seconds that lazily ticked away. Return journey to the city was devoid of all that I held within. Future held no meaning when I started from the city and now my past was also washed away as a faded memory of a story read somewhere. I felt a dark void, and the void was noisy, and painful. Do I also want to end up cracking like Antro? Maybe we always need a goal to chase, so we don't see life too closely. What can be that new goal? Where do I even look for any clues?

As it happens with such foolish questions, soon as they take clear shape in thought, the answer will be found already sitting in front of us, and staring intensly!

CHAPTER 4

Tolsi had noticed my cracking glaze soon after the journey began towards the city and my overtures in the inner void were perhaps too openly visible to those experienced eyes. Tolsi had been through a somewhat similar experience, albeit a few years prior. So what alternate goal did you find Tolsi? Isn't it apparent from the appearance?

Eyes had been looking at Tolsi all the time but they were not seeing. Maybe they were too busy feeling the inner turmoil and just appeared open on the outside. Indeed, Tolsi was on a path towards *the Ocean* that was said to behold all the truth of the universe and about which several messengers of olden times had talked about. As I recollected images and statues of these very messengers that were popular back home and those thick books that told unending tales about *the Ocean* and its zillions of glories.

Then I saw more clearly. Tolsi had washed off the glaze that city required on everyone, all the polish and colours that city demanded from its people, all the colourful dreams and ambitions and fantasies that city reinforced regularly and all the stiffness that one had to cultivate, to remain competitive and active. In fact Tolsi had even stopped being a porcelain doll! Tolsi had turned into a mud-ball, one that was always moist with joyful liquid, ready to adjust into any shape and just be one with the earth. A mud-ball that smelled of sacred fragrances, burst into the songs of *the ocean* and danced anytime, anywhere, perhaps in ecstasy. Or gratitude. For all I knew, it could even be due to the dark stuff Tolsi smoked often. But I was truly fascinated by this fellow! Hey, why is a sinking ship judging the colour of a helpful rescue boat? It just needs to tug on!

And tug-on I did, by following Tolsi on that long winding road to a place as mysterious as it gets.

◆ ◆ ◆

SECTION 2

Story of the mud-ball

The place Tolsi dwelled at was high up in the mountains, amidst virgin forests spread over an endless expanse, beyond several big and small streams that gushed down into great falls and often stopped for a brief while to kiss the rocks lying in their path, rocks that were simply idling and forever in wait. There were a few others too, all similar mud-balls, some with faces that changed as we talked, and shared a few common names that seem to call out from deep valleys and yet remained silent. Apparently whoever ventured into the people space would use the name Tolsi, so no one really was Tolsi.

They helped me rest and eat and washed away the cracking glaze that I had acquired in the city. They even helped with softening of the porcelain till I too became like them, a mud-ball, forever moist and fully capable of adjusting in any shape.

It was with them that I learned to wash away whatever it was that I called my past, although I had already witnessed the void it became. I was feeling fresh, flexible, relieved and full of useless energy, till they opened those learning chambers to my eager mind. The archives were full of ancient wisdom, written in many different hands, on many different material, mostly in forgotten languages and a few in a script that some adepts knew how to decipher. We just accepted that it was all wisdom contained in them and paid our reverences, but who knows! Whatever comes across or not, a mud-ball will adjust and take in.

That too I learnt in no time, but there really was no true concept of time, as it stretched out into an eternal day that alternated between light and darkness, as if a mother bird is gently flapping its wings over a bunch of hapless chicks, huddled up to conserve rapidly vanishing energy and hanging onto a meek thread of a hopeful future.

Not that I believed any future for the mud-balls! The

meaning and purpose of it all escaped my nascent understanding, though I surely had no interest in going back to where I came from, knowing fully well about the void it turned out to be amidst layers of confusion. We were always waiting for the visiting wise men, lovingly referred as Himba, as they too had no names. They would come at some intervals, tried to show us the keys to that deep secret explanation of *the ocean* that we all strived to see some day, although many of the Himba themselves seemed as far away from it as we, the local mud-balls.

Thin air in the mountains has many benefits, chiefly being a low supply of oxygen to the brain and so, pace of understanding suffers a great deal, which helps in keeping the simple lessons going on for a very long time and no one complaining about it. It also requires considerable effort in just being, so the dreams do not find it convenient to make their appearance and thus, mind remains devoid of useless clutter. Perhaps there goes the need to have a name or face. It was all so beautifully symbiotic that I easily lost track of time; Time which anyway had no meaning in those surroundings, except for the mundane business of the nature, which continued at its own pace, undisturbed.

Sometimes Himba would lead us into elaborate prayer rituals, reciting sacred hymns to invoke various incarnations of *the Ocean*, throwing select foods into the churning fire in the pit and ritualistic celebrations that continued for days at end. Another Himba would prescribe intense penances for each one of us, to test our individual willpower, tenacity, physical control on the body and knowledge of the deeper functioning of the body organs.

At times we had Himba go through the various meanings of scriptures with a fine-teeth comb, refining our understanding of them with extensive discussions that ran much into the nights and following days. Some of us were good at one kind of teachings and not so good at others, thus Himba would advise us to channel efforts accordingly. Peculiarly, when one of us mud-balls rose higher in a particular practice, somehow the mud would get moister and full of devine fragrance, just like we witnessed in every Himba. We also noticed that very old amongst us mud-balls would gradually dry up and finally crumble into fine dust one day. In fact, this happened so regularly that all of us remained alert and fearful of reaching the same end, without actually reaching anywhere closer to our chosen goal, of meeting *the Ocean*!

It wasn't too long before a Himba stopped by me and asked to meet privately, but since I lost all sense of time, it could've been after a very long time since my arrival there. Himba seemed pleased with something in me that was invisible to others before, perhaps my underlying restlessness or frustration, though I'd love to believe it was the abundant superior spiritual qualities lying untapped in me.

Over a course of few sessions, Himba explained how the mud-ball was simply the vessel to contain and facilitate journey of the essence, the moisture, which held the mud together and gave it an inner substance. And I learnt how to squeeze the moist essence out of the mud-ball, at will, into a tiny droplet!

This droplet then had freedom to become any form by moistening some dust and becoming a mud-ball. As a droplet, I could live forever, slipping from one mud-ball into another!

I was so thrilled with this 'achievement' that the fear of final drying out faded rapidly and I felt superior to all the other mud-balls. And I lost all interest in staying there any further, as a new desire, to help my old friends in the city, arose with extreme intensity.

Maybe I simply wanted to show off my ultimate stunt in the guise of philanthropy, who knows!

◆　◆　◆

SECTION 3

Story of the tiny droplet

Don't know what hit my senses more, the sudden explosion of mad activity or nostalgia of a bygone era, but I was flabbergasted soon as entering the big old city. As a mud-ball, I felt extremely vulnerable amongst all the glazed porcelain dolls zipping around constantly, but my confidence in the newly acquired inner secret was enough to keep me balanced, and slightly delighted. My second entry in this city was in fact entry of an entirely new being, though this time too there were some dreams playing under the flimsy demeanour, dreams of a different quality, and yet of somewhat similar desire.

City was very big, but for the first time I noticed that people lived in very tiny boxes. Not the size of their houses, but the size of the world they actually lived inside their heads. I knew it because I too was living in one such box, but that I didn't know back then. Coming from a prolonged stay in the mountains, all my senses were fresh and open to witness the box-world of others, and that was such an interesting but painfully boring realisation. The box was simply limited by the size of their sad realities, a handful of faces, a bunch of names, some scattered belongings and a whole lot of disappointments over the decisions they had made, the choices they believed were the most practical and a crazy amount of running in the mazes. All these boxes also had a long shadow of the ambitions people usually held and a generous smearing of hope to keep their world from crumbling under its own fault lines.

One by one, I connected with all the old names and dipped into their worlds briefly, for they were all the same. I could see their hidden sneer at how their friend had turned into a mud-ball, a sure sign of mental problems or perhaps this one was never meant to be a true city-zen. While they thought they had lot of new stories to tell and I had none, it's indeed funny how they really had nothing new or unique to tell and didn't have ears to listen to the astonishing new stuff I learnt in the mountains. As if we got separated by galactic distance in this brief or long period of my travel. There was nearly no overlap in theirs and my world, although I truly had no world of my own, since I was traveling as a Tolsi!

Most city folks have this tendency to eagerly convey the bad and worst information about common faces. Perhaps, seeing someone known fall or fail gives their own existence some solace, a relief to have escaped the fate's heavy hand and some faint confidence to carry on running inside their box world. Nitco, who had nudged me to take a break, was the one who cracked recently and falling apart alone, apparently having nowhere to go and no roots to go back to. Perhaps, that's why the nudge. Meanwhile, Antro had done a full circle and invested everything to establish an ashram, became a full-time guru for those who were about to crack, and was already a renowned one at that. I know it doesn't sound like a bad news, but when you see it as a mud-ball, it is a very bad news for the one's who were following Antro.

My eyes were looking for Posha and maybe also for all those tender and bitter-sweet moments we had together. Was I trying to grip something from that past to feel real, to add some solid fluff in the empty world of mine, to know that I was, and hence I am. Since I had moved to the mountains, Posha had truly moved on, and still moving on, rather leaping from one glazed doll to another, dolls higher up in hierarchy, dolls soaked up with more power, power to be the newsmaker in this big city, power to make and break lives, the same lives that people were living in their tiny boxes that had long shadows of ambition and some amount of hope smeared to hold up the cracks from breaking apart. Posha too had a harder exterior and glistening colourful new glaze, a fantastic presentation to the eyes of other porcelain dolls, perhaps as a symbol of their ambitious future and fruit of all the prayers to their favourite messengers of *the Ocean*, but it was such a sham to the eyes of a mud-ball, someone who had no name or face and yet being capable of eternal life.

When the past refuses to own up itself and the future has no ingredients to bake, it is the present moment that cares for one, a razor-thin cliff that doesn't let you fall but doesn't let you relax too. I had only my present in hand and that didn't offer much advice of where to go next, for one who has no inner box of world, no shadow of ambition – long or short, being anywhere is just the right place to be.

And so I moved, from being one mud-ball to another, squeezing out the essence as the old mud dried up, to enter into a new mud-ball, many times over, many-many times over. Thousands of different forms I took, several different terrains and several different experiences, and yet, they were all the same. In some time I noticed there were many others too who were moving with me, from one mud-ball to another, as if we were fellow travellers, and they seemed to enjoy it, just like I was enjoying initially, but then it all felt so pointless. Oh, wasn't this supposed to be the journey towards *the Ocean*? The one and only, that almighty one, the endless and ever-powerful, the ultimate source of all that is good, the merciful and the benefactor?

But where to find that one, thinking so I was watching a river flow towards an unknown destination, when this subtle voice came up from nearby. It was a drifting bubble on the shallow side of the river, shining brilliant rainbow colours as sunlight fell on its majestic dome, making gurgling sounds as it passed through whirlpools, delightful and happy! Seeing me in despair, it had stopped to pass on a message, maybe from someone who was watching it all, but it only asked me to drop this urge to live on in the mudball incarnations and let go in the river, as it was anyway going to meet *the Ocean* and all one had to do was to surrender to its currents.

Fear was back in my mind, but Ingus, as the bubble was named, said that only mud-balls are fearful of rivers, droplets ride on them as bubbles! And all such bubbles were called Ingus. It all sounded so natural and tempting that I went close to the stream, made the mud-ball squeeze for one last time and let the moisture droplet fall in the river. My moment of truth had arrived and the adviser was nowhere in sight. And magically, I was a bubble floating on the surface of the running river!

Indeed, mud-ball existence had its own charm but I was already well past that stage of craving for those charms, having lived through so many of them and yet not found an iota of memory to carry on this journey, the ride which I had already begun to enjoy, with bright sunlight hitting my dome and splitting into millions of colours, so bright and magical, I started regretting why I took so long to get on this journey! Now I had to do nothing, as the river was doing all that had to be done, to reach *the Ocean* and to be where everyone hoped to be some day.

◆ ◆ ◆

SECTION 4

Story of the bubble

I had a feeling of nearing the end of 'my' journey, as I knew myself, even though I went through a whole lot of shapes and names, before becoming this form. Freedom from the squishy mud and stiff porcelain and hard glaze and all that running around like a rat in a maze, was all behind me. I was light as the air! oh, but I indeed was largely some air trapped within water surface. Hey, but was I air or water now? Was I the moist essence who took so many forms or the lightly spread thin layer over a blob of air?

As I was drifting in these thoughts and drifting on the river all this while, I noticed many other bubbles floating around in the same direction. But some of them were drifting towards the riverbank! Curiously, some of them even got close to the shore and got back into a mud-ball form!! Ingus never told me this mystery so I had to ask the drifting ones. Well, some of them caught a new fear of getting annihilated upon reaching *the Ocean*, as no one ever came back to tell what happens beyond! A few of them wanted to linger on at the riverbank for digesting the fear, but rest of them decided to go back to their known world of being a mud-ball. Like me, they too actually had no real desire to be a mud-ball, having lived through enough times to know the futility of it, but they did have compassion for the others, those who were still seeking path to *the Ocean*, and they considered this as their call. At least till they figured out about going to that unknown beyond.

I was preparing myself for a dramatic climax of this journey and imagined how it would be to meet *the Ocean*, how I will share my stories from many lives and listen to what *Ocean* has to tell about the worlds of now and before and much before, and its many inhabitants, some alive and lot many who died before. Finally that moment arrived and the river opened its mouth to a mighty vast expanse of turquoise blue waters and said that this is as far as it can carry us and no further. Gently, most of us got moved from the sweet river water to the tastefully salty ocean, bobbing on the surface, looking in all directions and trying to figure out its reach, sharing our imaginations from the past and comparing if this indeed was *the Ocean* we were told about.

Curiously, all of us bubbles had travelled from different directions, had lived as different shaped mud-balls and porcelain dolls, had followed different religions and listened to different messengers, who had all spoken about *the Ocean* being one final destination for everyone, but here we were all the same, at exactly the same spot and in exactly the same form! So, was all that difference in our journeys just a false visual, a grand scheme devised by some cunning fellow mud-balls and dolls to keep us divided and fighting for righteousness of only their one preaching? How we argued and fought and criticised and spilled blood of our neighbours, just to convince them to realise folly of *their* practices and become a follower of what *we* believed in. In the end, did it matter what colour flag or dress or prayer hall we had? What rituals we followed, what messengers we believed in or what scriptures we read? All those differences now looked like a make-believe world that was struggling to make sense of its own existence and harming everyone else in the confusion.

My mind was buzzing with so many thoughts, visuals of all the different pasts I had and the people I found close enough to remember - **Chinook, Hatra, Ulgra, Timbro, Intok, Amphil, Posha, Antro, Nicto, Tolsi, Himba, Ingus** – At least till I lost track of time and interests in others. I felt like making *a garland of their initials*, just as a last token of my long story, a story that I will tastefully narrate *the Ocean*, when we talk.

But ocean was there and as silent as forever! I was in *the Ocean* and yet not able to communicate with it. No one told me the final trick of making this contact and no one seemed to go anywhere but kept bobbing on the surface. Soon I started aching with the pain of anxiety and separation from the one who knows it all and surely must be aware of my thoughts too. It was a pain because I was almost within reach and still far away, yet it was sweet, as I was almost within reach!

That one night was very long, very restless, very depressing and extremely dark. It was a night of all the nights I ever had in many lives and there wasn't even a tiny bit of hope of the morning. And then there was a dream, a dream where I was actually conversing with *the Ocean*, though it had no face or shape or substance and yet it appeared to be talking to me from all directions, including from my inside!

Surprisingly, there was no need to narrate my stories as *the Ocean* already knew each and every moment of various lives I had even things that I thought in private or tried hard to forget. Nothing was hidden from *the Ocean*, ever! And in that moment of my dumb silence *Ocean* revealed the secret last trick of meeting the final one. Just Pop! As simple as that!

Wait! If a bubble pops, then what remains of it?

Ocean kept smiling mysteriously and pretty soon it was morning.

First I considered sharing the dream with others bobbing around, but then decided against it. I wanted to test this first and perhaps then risk getting ridiculed by others. I took one last look around the beautiful morning sky, the colourful world that had been silent witness to the countless lives I went through since the time began. It all passed through behind the eyes, in a flash, as they say happens just before the moment of death. And this was perhaps my final death, or whatever it is called when a bubble pops.

One last look and POP..........

SECTION 5

Ocean at last!

Ha Ha Ha Ha Ha …….Ha Ha Ha Ha …….Ha Ha Ha Ha Ha… Ha Ha….

I had been laughing like mad for the longest time one could ever imagine. And then some more. It was all too hilarious to stay controlled.

Funny, it sounded like the noisy waves crashing the rugged shore, but it was all just my laughter. My belly was shaking wildly, appearing as the foamy waves, lapping around and rushing to the beach. It was just too much for me to hold in. This was truly unimaginable, even for someone like me who always had such a wild imagination!!!

Ho Ho Ho He he he....ha ha ha....

The Ocean that I had heard of from the devine messengers and those mystiques.... One that they all wished to meet some day in some life and what had eventually become my one goal in life... to meet the one and get all my questions answered... to meet personally...

POP!! When that scared bubble burst finally....

I was *the Ocean*!!!!

Correction! I was *the Ocean* all along, just didn't know it!

Right when I was a tiny droplet, squeezing from one mud-ball to another...

Right when I became a mud-ball and did all those compli-cated rituals in the mountains...

Right when I was sloshing around as a glazed porcelain doll in the big old city...

Even when I was a mischievous dull-white doll in that tiny hamlet!! I was always *the Ocean*!

Who told me? It's funny again, because all these answers are there hidden within my depths, all it needs is to peep below the rough surface....and as I recall those thousands of questions I had in many different forms, I just go down deep into my dark depths and answers appear!

Like, I know that not only was I *the Ocean* in all those forms I took, but also in every other form that I ever came across! All those adepts and city folks and hamlet friends... all the nameless and faceless people I didn't truly meet and yet, it was all me...

Not just the ocean and its waves, but also the air and clouds and mountains and forests and wells and streams and rocks and mud. You hear me in the gentle waves and the mighty ones; you hear me in the thunders and the breeze; you hear me in erupting volcanoes and the silent voices of the forests. You hear me everywhere and yet, you don't realize it's me.

I know it, because I too was you!

And who you believe you are, is nothing but I....

Now I know that living in the hamlet was only living in
the abject ignorance of the devine infinite. True, we lived
in synch with the nature, changing our lifestyle with sea-
sons and managing to survive through them. But we were
also acute witness to the cycle of nature that included
periodic destruction of the living and regeneration of the
new, death of our livestock and trees and the folks we
knew, as death was a constant visual in the hamlet. All of
us were scared of death and so, we used to conduct rituals
and prayed to a whole array of Godly figures, some more
popular than others. Fear of death decided how each one
organised their lives, but death was always just around the
corner. and life didn't have any grand scheme to follow,
just a few scattered moments of collective joys and griefs.

Now I know what we were chasing in our dreams, back
in the city. It looked like our dreams were full of hope
and elaborate plans of a glorious, endlessly happy exist-

ence, but it was all in some distant future. We were never content with the present and secretly ashamed of our individual past, so we joined the 'future dream industry' and jumped into the blind race.

But deep underneath, we were all seeking a comfort in something stable, something rock-solid, that wouldn't shake whatever be the force. Something that we could anchor onto and feel safe, feel in control. Safe from what we called as failure or dying with 'fate of a commoner' and its many different forms, that appeared as fears, as insecurity, as lust for achievement, as a constant drive to succeed, or at least find a mate and make babies, like our ancestors did, to keep the 'family name'. But at the root of all of them was one single 'truth', one inevitable event, called death. And however much we tried, whatever we did, failed or succeeded, it was always a failure, because death didn't spare anyone, ever.

Now I know that loss of hope drove us to abandon the city and head for the mountains, but what all of us mud-balls were trying to invoke, praying to and aspiring to achieve – was to go beyond that same death that took away even whatever was left with the nameless, faceless and shapeless mud-balls. Though we 'knew' that death is only end of one mud-ball existence and our 'soul' passes on to the next body, our one common fear was of failing to go beyond the unending cycle of birth-death before the present existence as a mud-ball dried up. The ultimate fear drove us to withdraw from the worldly life and practice severe austerity high up in the mountains.

When as a droplet I was squeezing from one mud-ball to another, and going through the same world of experiences in several life times, it was the same fear of reaching that dreadful end, which made me go on for so long. Talk of *the Ocean* was always that to me, just a talk, for I never truly believed any such almighty was there. I was only running away from the death, or at least trying to, though it was never too far behind.

Even as a bubble, that primal fear of being wiped out from 'existence', stayed back all along. For a very long time as a bubble, I was constantly riding the same ocean, and still afraid of my ridiculously tiny form, fearing to lose out – but lose what? Was that form the reality of my existence? Were any of those previous forms my reality?

Now I know, those were all the dreams of those individual forms that had relevance only within the dream, while the truth was silently participating all along, as if it had no intention of itself.

As an *Ocean* I know now that those 'dream lives' were boxed within tiny boundaries of time and space, with no escape into the truth. *Death*, rather fear of death, is my faithful agent that sometimes succeeds in making people stop and look for what lies behind the visible. *Hope* is my misguiding angel, which encourages them to keep on dreaming till they've reached maturity or hopelessness, whatever comes first. Together, they box them into a tightly-sealed dream zone and they continue going through cycles of re-manifestation, like rats running in a maze, hoping to find that cheese before they die of hunger or disappointment.

Wondering why *fear of death* a common theme across all forms of creation, even when they are periodically driven by hope? It is actually the intense fear of the unknown, the mysterious darkness that hides the truth behind the door of death. And an aspiration buried deep within everyone, to discover that truth. It takes several lifetimes for consciousness to get disillussioned from my misguiding angel, Hope, to bring this aspiration into the living reality, as it happened to me and other mud-balls who went to the mountains.

Now I know that every form I passed through, was like a glove that was constantly trying to hold things and people and thoughts and milestones and every other desire that it came across. But inside it was *the Ocean* that powered it all along, as also within all the others appearing on the outside.

You see, there is no other! Those are all the dreams that make us feel and believe to be different, as individuals, in our own private dream-world. When you finally wake up, it's all but one *Ocean*….and so it is all along.

What more is funny, is that *Ocean* is not even my name! How can you name that which is all, one and only? Who is there to name it and for what purpose, when there's no other? *Ocean* is the name given by some folks who managed to peep through their fantasy world and found me everywhere, and since they had to talk to you, they had to use some name, hence *the Ocean*. But that too got coloured by their less evolved disciples, who insisted upon only one true messenger, of course the one they were following, and thus so many different faiths came about. But don't you doubt, in each one of them, it is only I, for there truly is no other truth. Difference lies in the way they tried to uncover the hidden I, and so there are a million and more ways to reach here, to finally POP and become one with me.

So, now all I do is laugh and smile as I see those billions of forms sleep-walking in their dream-worlds and endlessly go through millions of lives. Sometimes they hear my laughter in the waves lapping the beaches or as thunder in the skies or as winds whistle through the trees and rivers gush down the mountains, but mostly they ignore me and stay engrossed in their dreams, till Hope finally leaves them or Death catches up with them, once again.

All of you are flowing in the same stream that runs into *the Ocean*. Often, people consider life as a challenge and that they have to fight and struggle to 'win' over it and also agree to suffer in the process. Even when they are trying to swim against the stream, that is true only in their ignorance, for everyone is flowing only in one direction, irrespective of what they do. Those who figure this out early, they let go off their imaginary 'I' and enjoy going with the flow. They are the ones who reach here faster, though everyone will eventually land up here and POP! Whatever you do, finally you would realise that you were always me, and then there shall be no Time or Space. So, go on sleeping as long as you wish, for that indeed is your only alternative.

Signing off here with the last few words.

I'm calling it an autobiography.

But no reason why it's mine only, it could easily be YOUR biography....

Actually it is, but you don't know it yet!